ICETE Series

Best Practice Guidelines for Doctoral Programs

ICETE International Council for Evangelical Theological Education
strengthening evangelical theological education through international cooperation

Langham
GLOBAL LIBRARY

I have carefully reviewed *Best Practice Guidelines for Doctoral Programs*, and was very impressed with their comprehensive coverage and perceptive articulation. The documents reflect the prevailing requirements of doctoral studies in high-quality institutions of higher education.

Wadi Haddad, PhD
President, Knowledge Enterprise
Editor-in-Chief, *TechKnowLogia*
Previously Chief of Education Division, World Bank

The *Best Practice Guidelines for Doctoral Programs* is a landmark document for evangelical scholarship. It is a document that unequivocally demonstrates that evangelicals are serious about academia. But it is also a document that unmistakably shows that academia must have a purpose that is bigger than an exercise of gaining knowledge as an end in itself. While firmly recognizing the validity of academic doctorates, the document equally recognizes the undoubted importance of professional doctorates. And yet, one can clearly see from the document that standards for both academic and professional doctorates are not designed in such a way that professional doctorates are gained through less rigorous processes than academic doctorates. Nor are they designed in such a way that those who earn the degrees are unable to engage with global scholarship and to converse with other scholars who earn their degrees in contexts other than those that are evangelically orientated. As an African working in an academic institution in Africa, I am absolutely delighted that these guidelines for doctoral programs have been prepared, because they will enable theological institutions on the continent, which have already started or plan to start doctoral programs, to have commonly agreed standards which can be used as a yardstick and reference when they develop their own standards and engage with accrediting bodies or institutions who might have their own standard documents.

Desta Heliso, PhD
Director, Ethiopian Graduate School of Theology (EGST)
Chair, Association for Christian Theological Education in Africa (ACTEA)

Many Majority World institutions have undertaken to provide higher-level degrees in theological education, including doctoral level. This document produced by ICETE after several global consultations provides benchmarks for excellence, for prospective doctoral scholars. This document provides world-recognized standards. It is my trust and hope that in future we will have Majority World scholars trained and rooted both in God's Word and excellent theological traditions, as well as engaged with the world – their own contexts. I highly commend that ICETE related institutions will uphold these benchmarks for the global Christians who will shape the thinking of the church and her involvement in God's mission.

Ashish Chrispal, PhD
Regional Director for Asia, Overseas Council, USA

Theological education needs scholars educated at the highest academic levels who will use their scholarship as expressions of the deepest levels of faithfulness to the mission of God for the church and the world. The ICETE *Best Practice Guidelines for Doctoral Programs* provides a thoughtful definition for quality in doctoral programs that meets this need precisely. The guidelines include a biblical and theological framework, as well as appropriate guidance for the educational, administrative, and resource requirements of doctoral programs. If implemented carefully by institutions accredited by ICETE member associations, the result will be a common doctoral education that will serve theological schools effectively. This is both a meaningful and significant document.

Daniel Aleshire, PhD
Executive Director,
The Association of Theological Schools (ATS), North America

Best Practice Guidelines for Doctoral Programs

Edited by
Ian J. Shaw
with
Scott Cunningham
Bernhard Ott

Series Editor
Riad Kassis

© 2015 by Ian J. Shaw

Published 2015 by Langham Global Library
an imprint of Langham Publishing
www.langhampublishing.org

Langham Publishing and its imprints are a ministry of Langham Partnership.

Langham Partnership
PO Box 296, Carlisle, Cumbria CA3 9WZ, UK
www.langham.org

ISBNs:
978-1-78368-080-1 Print
978-1-78368-082-5 Mobi
978-1-78368-081-8 ePub
978-1-78368-083-2 PDF

Ian J. Shaw has asserted his right under the Copyright, Designs and Patents Act, 1988 to be identified as the Author of this work.

All rights reserved. No part of this publication may be reproduced, stored in a retrieval system or transmitted, in any form or by any means, electronic, mechanical, photocopying, recording or otherwise, without the prior written permission of the publisher or the Copyright Licensing Agency.

Requests to reuse content from Langham Publishing are processed through PLSclear. Please visit www.plsclear.com to complete your request.

All scripture quotations, unless otherwise indicated, are taken from the Holy Bible, New International Version®, Anglicised, NIV® . Copyright © 1979, 1984, 2011 by Biblica, Inc.® Used by permission. All rights reserved worldwide.

British Library Cataloguing in Publication Data
A catalogue record for this book is available from the British Library

ISBN: 978-1-78368-080-1

Cover & Book Design: projectluz.com

Langham Partnership actively supports theological dialogue and a scholar's right to publish but does not necessarily endorse the views and opinions set forth, and works referenced within this publication or guarantee its technical and grammatical correctness. Langham Partnership does not accept any responsibility or liability to persons or property as a consequence of the reading, use or interpretation of its published content.

Contents

Foreword ix

Section 1

The Beirut Benchmarks. 1

Section 2

The Beirut Benchmarks Adaptation for
Professional Doctorates 3

Section 3

Best Practice Guidelines for Doctoral Programs 7
    I. Introduction 7
    II. Understanding the Nature of Research 10
    III. Key Principles for Best Practice in Doctoral Education 12

Details of ICETE Doctoral Initiative 51
    ICETE Doctoral Initiative Advisory Council 51
    ICETE Doctoral Initiative Steering Committee 52

With deep appreciation and gratitude to
Jim and Carolyn Blankemeyer and The Blankemeyer Foundation
for their unequivocal support for Majority World
doctoral theological education.

Foreword

One of the most significant and important trends within global theological education in our days is the increasing emergence of evangelical doctoral programmes in the Majority World.

In 2004, Dr Chris Wright, International Ministries Director of the Langham Partnership, drafted a discussion document on "Doctoral Scholarships in Majority World Institutions." At the International Council of Evangelical Theological Education's 2006 international consultation in Chiang Mai, Thailand, he proposed the need for an international consultation for these emerging doctoral programmes in the evangelical Majority World.

ICETE's international director at that time, Dr Paul Sanders, began exploratory discussions with Dr Chris Wright and Dr David Baer of Overseas Council (OC) about the feasibility of an ICETE Doctoral Initiative. Both international bodies agreed to support such an initiative.

ICETE established an Oversight Committee to assist in developing the ICETE Doctoral Initiative, consisting of representatives from global institutions already offering doctoral programs, namely: the late Dr Douglas Carew (AIU/NEGST Kenya), *chair*; and Drs Carver Yu (CGST Hong Kong); Oscar Campos (SETECA Guatemala); Theresa Lua (AGST Philippines); and Paul Sanders (ICETE) *ex officio*. This group met for the first time in Sopron, Hungary, in October 2009.

The ICETE Doctoral Initiative was then formally launched with a planning consultation held in March 2010 in Beirut, Lebanon. The event involved a selected list of key institutions offering doctoral programs in the Majority World, who were together representative of the larger movement. The Beirut 2010 consultation explored a wide range of relevant interests. It also devised and unanimously adopted a statement on excellence in doctoral programs, titled the *Beirut Benchmarks*.

A second planning consultation was held in October 2011 in Bangalore, India. The gathering unanimously adopted the *Bangalore Affirmations*. It also approved an adaptation of the *Beirut Benchmarks for Professional Doctorates*. The third ICETE Doctoral Consultation took place in October 2012 in Nairobi, Kenya.

In 2013, Dr Riad Kassis, ICETE's current international director, worked to form an Advisory Council and a Steering Committee to carry the ICETE Doctoral Initiative forward. A complete list of the members of the Advisory Council and the Steering Committee is provided at the end of this document as an appendix.

The following documents have been produced for the benefit of doctoral programs in theological disciplines wherever they are offered by evangelical institutions, whether in the Majority World or in the West. They arise out the above-mentioned consultations attended by invited delegates from ICETE, Langham Partnership, and Overseas Council, as well as a range of academic leaders from the Majority World. They have been prepared to assist the enhancement of current and emerging doctoral programs globally. They explain and amplify the core documents agreed upon at those consultations – *The Beirut Benchmarks* and *The Beirut Benchmarks adaptation for Professional Doctorates* – and provide guidelines for how these core principles can be applied. These Best Practice Guidelines are written to assist all doctoral programs in their aspiration for continuous improvement. In some countries the doctoral studies of evangelical students are not conducted in the context of evangelical seminaries, but instead in the secular university setting with supervision from an evangelical doctoral supervisor. In such cases some of the standards outlined in these guidelines may not apply directly. Nonetheless the spirit and key principles of the documents can also readily be applied in these contexts.

I would like to offer thanksgiving to God for his grace that enabled the formation of these significant documents. I would like also to express my gratitude to those who spent efforts and sleepless nights on them. In particular, I would like to mention Dr Ian Shaw, Dr Paul Bowers, Dr Scott Cunningham, and Dr Bernhard Ott.

Rev Riad Kassis, PhD
International Director, International Council for Evangelical Theological Education
Director, Langham Scholars Ministry, Langham Partnership

Section 1

The Beirut Benchmarks

Doctoral study within an evangelical Christian institution is founded on an understanding of knowledge that is more than academic. In the Bible, acquiring and exercising wisdom involves a combination of faith, reason and action. It requires

- right belief and committed trust in the living God ("the fear of the LORD is the first principle of wisdom"),
- creative and humble use of the rationality God has granted to humans made in his own image, and
- appropriate living in the world to reflect God's calling and participate in God's mission.

Doctoral study, therefore, pursued on such a foundation, will be *confessional*, *rational* and *missional*. For a Christian, doctoral study is one dimension of what it means to "love the LORD your God with all your heart and mind and soul and strength."

Within such a framework of Christian identity and commitment, the doctoral qualification will be awarded to students who are church members commended for faithful discipleship and recognized leadership, and who demonstrate the following qualities through appropriate examination:

1. <u>Comprehensive understanding</u>, having demonstrated a breadth of systematic understanding of a field of study relevant to the Christian community of faith, and mastery of the skills and methods of research appropriate to that field.

2. <u>Critical skills, faithfully exercised</u>, having demonstrated their capacity for critical analysis, independent evaluation of primary and secondary source materials, and synthesis of new and

inter-related ideas through coherent argumentation, and their commitment to exercise such skills on the foundation of biblical faithfulness to Jesus Christ and his church.

3. <u>Serious inquiry with integrity</u>, having demonstrated the ability to conceive, design and implement a substantial project of inquiry resulting in a sustained and coherent thesis, and to do so with Christian and scholarly integrity.

4. <u>Creative and original contribution</u>, having produced, as a result of such disciplined inquiry, a creative and original contribution that extends the frontiers of knowledge, or develops fresh insights in the articulation and contextual relevance of the Christian tradition, some of which merit national or international refereed publication.

5. <u>Contextual relevance</u>, having shown their capacity, in the course of their doctoral program and in their expectation of its future potential, for biblically-informed critical engagement with the realities of their cultural contexts.

6. <u>Ability to communicate</u>, having shown an ability in communicating about their area of expertise to peer-level academic audiences, and, where appropriate, to non-specialists in local Christian communities and the wider society in culturally relevant ways, including their mother tongue, for example through teaching, preaching or writing.

7. <u>Missional impact</u>, having shown that they are committed, and can be expected, to use the fruit of their doctoral study, the skills it has given them and the opportunities it affords them, to promote the kingdom of God and advance the mission of the church (both local and global), through Christ-like and transformational service, to the glory of God.

Endorsed unanimously on 6 March 2010
by the participants in the ICETE Doctoral Consultation
Beirut, Lebanon

Section 2

The Beirut Benchmarks Adaptation for Professional Doctorates

The Professional Doctorate in an aspect of Christian ministry is a doctoral level qualification, which utilizes the professional, ministerial practice of the candidate as a part of the structured process of learning. The practice-based setting of the student is a central component of the research project. In the professional doctorate, the student works from both theory and practice, towards enhanced competencies for both the individual and the wider profession. The holder of a Professional Doctorate in Christian ministry is therefore a researching professional, extending the boundaries of reflective practice in an area of Christian ministry.

Doctoral study within an evangelical Christian institution is founded on an understanding of knowledge that is more than academic. In the Bible, acquiring and exercising wisdom involves a combination of faith, reason and action. It requires:

- right belief and committed trust in the living God ("the fear of the LORD is the first principle of wisdom"),
- creative and humble use of the rationality God has granted to humans made in his own image, and
- appropriate living in the world to reflect God's calling and participate in God's mission.

Doctoral study, therefore, pursued on such a foundation, will be *confessional*, *rational* and *missional*. For a Christian, doctoral study is one dimension of what it means to "love the LORD your God with all your heart and mind and soul and strength."

Within a framework of Christian identity and commitment, the *professional* doctoral qualification will be awarded to students who are *church members, and are recognised and experienced practitioners in Christian ministry,* commended for faithful discipleship and recognized leadership, and who *have demonstrated* the following qualities through appropriate examination *and peer-level professional review*:

1. <u>Comprehensive understanding,</u> having demonstrated a breadth of systematic understanding of a field of study *at the forefront of professional practice in an aspect of Christian ministry,* mastery of the skills and methods of research, *and applied reflective-practice in a specific ministry context.*

2. <u>Critical skills, faithfully exercised,</u> having demonstrated their capacity for independent evaluation of primary and secondary source materials, *and practice-based research. Students must show ability to maintain an appropriate critical distance from their own professional context, and capacity to integrate academic knowledge and professional practice at doctoral level. A commitment to exercise such skills* on the foundation of biblical faithfulness to Jesus Christ and his Church must be demonstrated.

3. <u>Serious inquiry with integrity,</u> *having* demonstrated the ability to conceive, design and implement a substantial project of *research into, and critical analysis of, current and previous professional practice, and* ability to generate mutual critique with thinkers and practitioners from outside their immediate ministry context, resulting in a sustained and coherent thesis, and to do so with Christian and scholarly integrity.

4. <u>Creative and original contribution,</u> having produced, as a result of such disciplined inquiry, a creative and original contribution that - a) extends the frontiers of knowledge, b) *generates new perspectives, approaches or paradigms in professional practice, and c) enhances the integration between theological reflection and Christian ministry practice,* and so merits *publication in* national or international *professional literature.*

5. <u>Contextual relevance,</u> having shown their capacity, in the course of their doctoral program and in their expectation of its future potential, for biblically-informed critical engagement *and enhanced and applied professional practice within* the realities of their cultural contexts.

6. <u>Ability to communicate,</u> having shown an ability in communicating about their area of expertise to peer-level academic *and professional* audiences. Where appropriate this communication should be to non-specialists in local Christian communities and the wider society in culturally relevant ways, including their mother tongue, for example through teaching, preaching or writing.

7. <u>Missional impact,</u> having shown that they are *committed, able and can be expected to* use the fruit of their doctoral study, *and* the skills it has given them and the opportunities it affords them, to promote the kingdom of God and advance the mission of the church (both local and global) *through significant enhancement of theory and of professional practice* in transformational service and Christ-like leadership, to the glory of God.

Endorsed unanimously on 14 October 2011
by the participants in the ICETE Doctoral Consultation
Bangalore, India

Section 3

Best Practice Guidelines for Doctoral Programs

I. Introduction

Best practice is something that Christians should strive for in all dimensions of living. It is part of the integrated Christian life, a holistic response to the needs and challenges of each context in which we worship and work. In 2 Corinthians 8:7 Paul commends the Corinthians for how they "excel in everything", including "in faith, in speech, in knowledge, in complete earnestness and in your love for us". So the aspiration of all theological educators must be to "excel in everything".[1] Excellence in the creation and delivery of programs of theological education has a biblical mandate.

Best practice is needed to safeguard academic standards and ensure successful delivery by theological institutions in the evangelical tradition of doctoral programs to national and international expectations. This should be done in such a way that those engaged in doctoral study are spiritually formed by the process and equipped for God-honouring service.

These Best Practice Guidelines develop the implications of what is set out in the *Beirut Benchmarks* and the *Beirut Benchmarks Adaptation for Professional Doctorates*. They serve in the way that 'Deuteronomy' does to

---

1. 2 Corinthians 8:7, "just as you excel in everything – in faith, in speech, in knowledge, in complete earnestness and in your love for us – see that you also excel . . ."; Philippians 4:8, "if anything is excellent or praiseworthy – think about such things." The ultimate purpose for the pursuit of excellence is the glory of God (1 Cor 10:31), not just excellence for its own sake as an end in itself.

the 'Decalogue'. They are designed both to establish expectations, illustrate how the *Beirut Benchmarks* can be applied, and also to serve as a tool of analysis to encourage ongoing reflection on best practice. They seek to set out global principles for best practice, and are not simply addressed from one community to other communities. These guidelines are designed as much for seminaries and Christian universities in the West as for those in the Majority World.

The excellence in best practice we strive for must be credible. It needs to be capable of being assessed by measurable benchmarks, so that institutions can reflect on their performance and constantly strive to do better. In this endeavour, academic excellence is a non-negotiable. But we also need to have a fuller and more comprehensive understanding of excellence than one that is solely academic. With the global growth of doctoral programs, there is increased pressure for international 'harmonization' of qualifications. Because the doctorate is a global product, it must conform to certain global expectations and standards, matching up to key global reference points. For example, the Bologna process in the European Higher Education Area is already setting standards and creating pressures for conformity that are being felt well outside Europe. The need to be credible and achieve national government recognition for doctoral programs means this issue is no longer a debate confined to the West. Many national bodies across the world are also looking to Bologna for benchmarks. In the 2010 ICETE doctoral consultation in Beirut, it was decided to consider the Dublin Descriptors (produced for 'D' level awards as part of the Bologna process) as a starting point for an understanding of internationally accepted standards of doctoral education, and to develop and enhance them with a distinctively Christian philosophy of education. This need for parameters for doctoral programs offered by theological institutions in the evangelical tradition, understood and accepted in Asia, Europe, Africa, North and South America, and Australasia lies behind the *Beirut Benchmarks* that emerged from those discussions.

This does not mean all doctoral programs should be exactly the same. There will be contextual variety in a number of areas. Yet the final product still needs to look like a doctorate and be recognized as such in the eyes of the global academic community, as well as by local accreditors or validators, churches, and students undertaking the program. It should be delivered to the highest standards of Best Practice. There is as yet no higher earned academic award than the doctorate, although some offer differing classifications within the doctoral award itself (such as Laude, Magna Cum Laude, etc). The very nature of the doctorate demands excellence of those who offer it. But alongside this, leaders of evangelical theological institutions need to challenge themselves to make the doctorate the pinnacle of Christian training. It should be seen as the place where we seek to be most excellent in preparing Christian leaders for service.

Institutions offering the doctoral award need to do so with the right motivations. Similarly, candidates on doctoral programs should undertake them with the right motivations. As Andrew Walls has recently written:

> It is necessary to begin by distinguishing between promoting scholarship and producing PhDs. In every continent there are already enough holders of doctorates who have never contributed a jot or tittle to scholarship. There is no point in setting up factories in Africa and Asia, however efficient, to train people to jump through doctoral hoops who have no calling for scholarship and no passion (for nothing less will do) for its exercise. The pursuit of the scholarly life is a Christian vocation within God's mission to the world; in comparison with this, the quest for doctorates is frivolity.[2]

Striving for excellence in the delivery of doctoral programs means the institution must be a 'learning' community, not just a community where learning takes place. Those involved in Christian education need to strive always to do better; to be more Christ-like in how things are done; to be more biblical in their guiding principles; and ever more desirous of higher standards. Institutions always need to evaluate practice, face up to mistakes, and learn from them.

---

2. Andrew Walls, "World Christianity, Theological Education and Scholarship," *Transformation*, Vol 28, no. 4 (2011): 235–240.

II. Understanding the Nature of Research

Research has traditionally been understood as original investigation undertaken in order to gain knowledge and understanding. It includes the generation of ideas; the development of projects that lead to new or improved insights; and the use of knowledge to produce new or improved materials, processes, and designs. At its heart lies scholarship, which involves the creation, development, and maintenance of the intellectual infrastructure of a subject or discipline.

The core skills in scholarship are *consolidation, discovery, integration, and application*.

- **Consolidation** is rooted in the awareness of the breadth of research that has taken place before a project begins, the foundation upon which our own scholarship takes place. It requires the understanding, analysis and synthesis of prior research and its implications for current study and contexts.
- **Discovery** involves a desire to find out new things, devise new arguments, or explore documents and sources that have not previously been read and investigated. It is driven by a desire to see an issue or problem more clearly. Old material can be viewed in a fresh way.
- **Integration** flows from discovery. It involves the making of connections, and building bridges to current knowledge and exploring the implications of this. In some cases this kind of study can lead to new hypotheses and conclusions. In others it can confirm existing conclusions, though it may do so in new ways.
- Research should be **disseminated and applied**. It should not only address areas pertinent to current academic debate, but also serve the needs of the wider Christian community. It should also be connected to the pedagogical needs of the seminary. From research should follow stimulating, creative, and effective approaches to teaching and learning, and dissemination of research findings.

Research Is Something That Should Excite Evangelicals, and Be Warmly Embraced for Its Potential.

Research is part of loving God with the mind (Matt 22:37–40).

The emphasis on 'newness' does not imply that research necessarily entails a challenge to biblical or confessional orthodoxy. Research can be legitimately seen as a way of both creating new paradigms where they are needed, but also of enhancing former ones based on a conviction of biblical authority, a distinctly Christian worldview, and confessional orthodoxy.

Researchers should be both trailblazers of new thinking, and also renovators and restorers of core kingdom values and the building blocks of spiritual formation

Research Should Be Done for the Glory of God

Christian scholars should learn how to be humble and cautious about the findings of their research. Scholarship will be tested and evaluated by others, and this ongoing scholarly process should be welcomed, even when this means earlier findings need to be re-evaluated.

The controlling desire of the researcher must be the desire to bring glory to God through research, just as through any other part of Christian ministry. Prayer should accompany this process of seeking insight. God alone should get all the credit for the insights he brings.

III. Key Principles for Best Practice in Doctoral Education

1) Doctoral Studies Undertaken in an Evangelical Context Should Be Founded on a Truly Christian Understanding of Knowledge and Wisdom

At the heart of doctoral programs in evangelical theological institutions should be a genuinely Christian philosophy of education. This will mean that doctoral studies undertaken in an evangelical seminary or university will have the same academic rigor and standards as those in a secular university, but will be based on different foundational principles. This is expressed at the beginning of the *Beirut Benchmarks*. Knowledge is more than simply gaining possession of large amounts of information –"In the Bible, acquiring and exercising wisdom involves faith, reason and action."

Doctoral study is therefore a faith exercise, as well as a mental exercise. "The beginning of wisdom is the fear of God." (Prov 9:10) As the *Beirut Benchmarks* indicate, this wisdom "requires right belief and committed trust in the living God".

This means that doctoral education is *confessional* – it draws on personal and community faith values. This confessional [3] basis provides the firm foundation for research, but this does not need to place a limit on research. This faith exercise is not to be separated from the mind, as the *Beirut Benchmarks* stress, it requires the "creative and humble use of the rationality God has granted to humans made in his own image". Thinking profoundly about the things of God is part of worship – we are to love the Lord our God with all our heart and soul and mind (Matt 22:37). It is one part of the proper exercise of spiritual disciplines.

Doctoral study needs to be understood holistically. It is an extension into another dimension of the candidate's Christian experience, and because of this the characteristics of integrity and integration are required.

With these principles in mind the experience of doctoral education in a theological seminary or Christian university will be notably different to similar work in a secular institution. A doctoral program should be as

---

3. This is 'confession' with a small c, and is not limited to one particular Confession.

academically excellent as any offered in a secular institution, but this should be combined with a fully rounded understanding of knowledge and wisdom, establishing for the believer a rich and fulfilling context in which excellence in academic and spiritual disciplines is consciously nurtured.

2) Doctoral Education in Evangelical Theological Institutions Should Have the Bible as Its Foundation

In evangelical theological institutions the centrality of the Word of God should be the point of reference for all theological reflection. This does not mean that the Bible is the only topic studied. However, the study of the Bible as the core discipline of Christian theology should permeate all other fields of theological study and their application. This is well expressed by the *Cape Town Commitment* (2010): "Theological education serves first to train those who lead the church as pastor-teachers, equipping them to teach the truth of God's Word with faithfulness, relevance and clarity; and second to equip God's people for the missional task of understanding and relevantly communicating God's truth in every cultural context."[4]

Therefore, doctoral education in evangelical contexts should be one dimension of this greater goal of equipping Christian leaders for faithfully reading, interpreting, and proclaiming the Bible – as Paul wrote of the role of the Overseer in Titus 1:9. "He must hold firmly to the trustworthy message as it has been taught, so that he can encourage others by sound doctrine and refute those who oppose it."[5]

Those who make decisions about the admissions of students onto doctoral programs, and those assessing research proposals from potential students, should consider this dimension, and encourage students to keep this greater

---

4. *Cape Town Commitment, Call to Action* (Peabody: Hendrickson - Didasko Files, 2011), F4, D, 69–70.

5. See also 2 Timothy 4:1–2: "In the presence of God and of Christ Jesus, who will judge the living and the dead, and in view of his appearing and his kingdom, I give you this charge: preach the Word; be prepared in season and out of season; correct, rebuke and encourage." 1 Timothy 4:13: "Devote yourself to the public reading of Scripture, to preaching and to teaching." Titus 1:9: "He [an Overseer] must hold firmly to the trustworthy message as it has been taught, so that he can encourage others by sound doctrine and refute those who oppose it." Titus 2:1: "You must teach what is in accord with sound doctrine."

goal in mind from the outset, without limiting the academic freedom of enquiry needed in the research process.[6]

3) Doctoral Studies in Theological Disciplines Should Be Missional[7]

As is expressed in the *Beirut Benchmarks*, doctoral education in theological studies should be designed *to "promote the kingdom of God and advance the mission of the church (both local and global)"*. Theological education itself is an essential aspect of mission; serving the mission of the church in the world, as Paul wrote in 2 Timothy 2:2. "The things you have heard me say in the presence of many witnesses entrust to reliable men who will also be qualified to teach others."[8]

Providing high-grade theological education at doctoral level is also an aspect of the Christ's lordship being reflected at all levels of theological education, in continuity with 2 Corinthians 10:4–5. "We take captive every thought to make it obedient to Christ."[9] Theological education in the evangelical tradition involves mission *as* the academy – through deploying the full resources of Christians working in the scholarly community in the task of mission.

But evangelical theological education also has a role of mission *to* the academy – providing a distinctively Christian voice within global academic

---

6. Even in fields that are not directly 'biblical studies', this should be encouraged. Projects in theology, missiology, church history, and practical theology can raise questions as to how the Bible has been or is currently preached, interpreted, practiced. Study of other religions can be taken with the motivation to equip students to relate the message of the Bible to other faith communities. This component of biblical reflection can prevent projects from becoming solely philosophical or anthropological.

7. By missional we do not mean exclusively focused on 'mission studies' as a narrowly defined discipline. Missional instead refers to the orientation of the overall doctoral program, and is used in its holistic sense. For a full understanding of 'missional' see *The Cape Town Commitment*; C. J. Wright *The Mission of God* (Leicester: IVP, 2006); Samuel T. Logan, ed., *Reformed Means Missional: Following Jesus into the World* (Greensboro: New Growth Press, 2013).

8. Colossians 1:28–29: "We proclaim him, admonishing, and teaching everyone with all wisdom, so that we may present everyone perfect in Christ. To this end I labour, struggling with all his energy, which so powerfully works in me."

9. 2 Corinthians 10:4–5: "The weapons we fight with are not the weapons of the world. On the contrary, they have divine power to demolish strongholds. We demolish arguments and every pretension that sets itself up against the knowledge of God, and we take captive every thought to make it obedient to Christ."

discourse that needs to be heard and taken into account. Christian scholars from both the Majority World and the West have a unique opportunity to engage with, and help shape, current theological trajectories. Doctoral education helps equip Christian scholars to engage in this vital work of mission to and within the academy, enabling them to bring a distinctive and intellectually credible response to key debates from an evangelical perspective. Doctoral scholars from the Majority World have especial insights and cultural and theological perspectives that scholars in the West need to hear, and vice versa.

The Christian calling, or vocation, to be a theological educator should be recognized and honoured. John Calvin spoke of the role of the *doctor ecclesiae*, the Doctor of the Church (Calvin, *Institutes* 4:3). Andrew Walls reminds us that "The pursuit of the scholarly life is a Christian vocation within God's mission to the world."[10] So, in their rationale and motivation, doctoral programs should ultimately be missional, provided with the intention of contributing to the extension of God's kingdom in the world.

4) Doctoral Studies Should Be Done in Community

The important role that community plays in the formation of scholars should be recognized in doctoral programs. Traditional doctoral programs saw a single researcher working with a single supervisor/mentor, a model that often fostered a sense of isolation, loneliness, and individualism. Programs that are designed to produce not only academic excellence, but also genuine spiritual formation, should address the ways in which a learning community of scholars can be created, one that will support, encourage, and challenge all its members. The creation of a mutually supportive learning community should be an important aim of doctoral programs, and represents a significant element in the scholar's spiritual formation.[11]

Although most doctoral research projects in theology are individual, they are best carried out in a context of community, where learners are accountable to, and supportive of, each other. Those programs with a coursework and

---

10. Walls, "World Christianity."
11. Acts 2:42: "They devoted themselves to the apostles' teaching and to the fellowship, to the breaking of bread and to prayer."; Acts 17:11: "They received the message with great eagerness and examined the Scriptures every day to see if what Paul said was true."

seminar-based period of study at their start are often better equipped to foster community than those that do not.

Learning developed in community and with a sense of mutual service lessens the dangers of individualism and loneliness that often characterize doctoral programs. The scholarly community is where the doctoral student learns the practice of peer review, critique and academic dialogue, and the skills of being a steward of the discipline. Working towards academic and spiritual formation in community, and through cohort learning [whether formally assessed or not], should be encouraged in doctoral education. Programs have successfully created community by hosting regular (monthly or more frequent) research seminars at which students and faculty present work; others hold annual or biannual residential research colloquiums for their doctoral students, attendance at which is a required part of the program. The creation of mutually supportive prayer ministry, fellowship and Bible study groups, and holding social gatherings for scholars, are also effective means of fostering community.

Those programs which are offered 'at a distance', or with 'flexible access', need to be creative in fostering a sense of community. By means of emerging technologies and communications, research seminars and discussion groups can be held, online debates and blogs conducted, and virtual community created.

The values of community learning and support should be embraced by all members of the institution: students, faculty and all other staff. Special efforts should be made to ensure that non-residential, part-time, and at-a-distance students are thoroughly integrated into the learning community.

Doctoral students need to recognize that this sense of community should extend to participation in the local Christian community. Any sense of disconnection between the academic world and the local church should be avoided. Doctoral studies are undertaken for the greater glory of God and to serve the wider church. Doctoral students need to integrate their academic formation with the faithful practice of everyday spiritual disciplines and engagement with local Christian church community.

5) Individual Doctoral Programs Should Remain Connected with Others That Operate within the Global Educational Community

As evangelical theological education grows in its extent and diversity, there is an increased need for mutual accountability, comparability and convertibility of theological education qualifications. Programs should seek to understand and articulate a Christian understanding of quality and excellence, and not solely rely on definitions from secular and governmental authorities. This requires serious theological reflection to ensure that quality is measured in ways that serve both the needs of the academic community and of churches in their witness and service. The ICETE doctoral process, which brought together representatives of the global theological academic community and through which the *Beirut Benchmarks* were produced, is a significant step in this process.

Doctoral programs in the global academic community need to learn from each other in developing fresh understandings of what constitutes excellence in the delivery of doctoral education. This means taking account of the realities of the lives of scholars with their different learning styles, potential modes of delivery of course content and supervision, without diminishing the requirement for the PhD to remain the pinnacle of academic achievement. Partnerships between seminaries in the Majority World and the rest of the world should be developed, allowing for flexible ways of accessing the best resources and bringing them within the reach of Majority World programs, and bringing a global awareness and dimension to programs in the West. Partnerships developed need to be founded on mutual respect and support, with a genuine desire to enhance local programs and without the imposition of dominant models from outside contexts. Theological educators in the West need to learn humbly and graciously from best practice in the Majority World.

There is a need for genuinely global, not just bi-lateral, partnerships, as Andrew Walls has observed:

> Our present context calls us to develop multilateral relations across the world, and theological education has everything to gain from the development of interactions between Africa and Asia and Latin America. There are even broad similarities in

theological issues that arise from the worldviews of Africa, the tribal peoples of India, Myanmar and Thailand, the mountain and forest peoples of the Americas, and the island peoples of the Pacific, that need to be discussed within a single forum, and not simply in regional terms.[12]

This Global-South to Global-South conversation is a key and growing part of this global theological conversation, and ensures individual doctoral programs remain connected to the wider global academic network.

6) Doctoral Programs Should Be Relevant to Context

Each doctoral program resides in a local **cultural and educational setting**.

The Local Educational Context

This is an important consideration for every doctoral program whether in the Majority World or in the West. Meeting the standards of the government of the region – in terms of accreditation or validation – is crucial. As the Bologna process has taken hold, government bodies across the Majority World are increasingly looking to the Bologna benchmarks – and demanding high standards before programs are licensed or accredited. Others look to different international accreditation standards. Doctoral programs need to reflect both national and international standards and expectations.

The Local Church Context

Doctoral programs should serve the needs of the church community as an aspect of transformational service. Those who are to be equipped to participate in God's mission in the world need to be prepared through the learning that is both rooted in and responsive to the culture and context. Theological education should equip God's people "for the missional task of understanding and relevantly communicating God's truth in every cultural context".[13]

Students need to be able to apply a Christ-centred worldview in the areas of learning, researching, and writing, in order to make knowledge and

---

12. Walls, "World Christianity."
13. *Cape Town Commitment*, Section 2: F; 4, p. 69.

research both faithful to the mission of God and responsive to the needs of both the local region and the world.

Each doctoral program should be sensitive to local cultural context. Efforts should be made to encourage research into issues that are relevant to the context in which it is undertaken.[14] Doing theology in context does not mean every project becomes a facet of practical theology, for example, there is a place for high-grade skills in Hebrew, Greek, Bible exegesis and hermeneutics to equip faculty who can teach to an advanced level in those areas.

When helping students select their research topics, they need to be encouraged to ask the question – how does this serve not only the needs of scholarship, but of the local context? Efforts should be made to avoid the uncritical transplanting of theologies from other contexts that are not relevant or helpful in that local situation. Research that is relevant to context can take many forms. Context informs the questions and areas explored by students. Even what appear the most purely biblical and theological topics can arise in response to issues in context. More applied disciplines (such as Practical Theology or Intercultural Studies) may provide more direct implications for the context, but in every discipline contextual relevance should play a role in the research undertaken and the motivation for it.

Theological education needs to be responsive, culturally sensitive and contemporary, without losing its traditional focus on the core disciplines of Biblical Studies, Theology, Church History, Systematic Theology, Ethics, Mission and Pastoral Theology.

However, learning should not be compartmentalized, and the value of interdisciplinary study needs to be recognized, preparing students for the complex realities of public ministry.

Students need to be globally aware of scholarly perspectives on the research subject, and able to relate their work to other contexts. But alongside this, the riches of the local context can be brought to the core discipline. This can mean exploring local primary source research materials. The experiences of local communities can also serve as a hermeneutical tool, opening up fresh perspectives on biblical, theological, missiological and historical materials, in

---

14. These will vary considerably, but where issues such as poverty, materialism, violence, lack of educational opportunity, corruption, ethnic conflict, inter-religious hostility, or injustice are features of life, biblically informed research should be encouraged to equip local churches with how to respond.

a way that approaches solely taken from the West are unable to do. Andrew Walls stressed this:

> Africa, Asia and Latin America must first become centres of creative thinking, world leaders in biblical and theological studies. . . . For the sake of the Christian Church worldwide, Africa, all Asia and Latin America, home to so many Christians, must pull their true theological weight.[15]

7) Doctoral Programs Must Ensure That Students Are Fully Able to Engage with Global Academic Discourse

It is important that doctoral programs introduce students to the full range of cutting-edge global academic discourse in their chosen research field. This will provide them with breadth and enrichment of learning and cross-fertilization of ideas, as well as ensuring the international comparability of their award.

Students need access to the full range of global literature in their chosen discipline. This needs to be reflected in the library and electronic learning resources to which they have access.

- It is particularly valuable when doctoral programs arrange for students to undertake a portion of the program in an academic setting outside their own regional context in a location where learning resources are particularly strong. This brings a breadth of access to library and archival resources, as well as a richness of research exposure to other scholars, and the range of global academic discourse. Doctoral students in both the Majority World and the West should also be encouraged to gain research exposure outside their immediate context.
- Doctoral students should be encouraged to take opportunities to present and discuss their research work at peer-level with other doctoral students, as well as in regional, national and international conferences in their subject fields.
- Doctoral programs should seek to introduce their doctoral students to a range of academic perspectives from scholars at the cutting

---

15. Walls, "World Christianity," 238.

edge of global academic research. This can be facilitated through the invitation of international academic specialists to speak at research conferences, to deliver seminar components, and through their engagement as second supervisors, second readers of theses, and as external examiners.

8) Doctoral Programs Should Ensure the Integration of Academic Skills Formation and Spiritual Formation

Doctoral programs should help students to see the connection between research and spiritual formation. This means that doctoral students should seek God's help in all aspects of their lives and their education.

Scholars should be produced who are able to integrate both academic and spiritual excellence, working to the higher end of the transformation of the whole people of God according to the image of Christ and his mission in the world. Doctoral programs should produce researchers who are faithful both to the Word of God and to the demands of their discipline, and also theological teachers who demonstrate a spirituality that impacts heart, hands and mind.

Program Design

Doctoral programs should be constructed in such a way that any separation between the academic discipline and the rest of life, which too often characterizes advanced studies, is avoided.

The Practice of Research

In doctoral research, students should actively deploy the Christian disciplines in all aspects of their work. They should learn to treat sources with care, faithfully recording and representing them. Integrity in handling the intellectual property and argumentation of others is part of a Christian commitment to truthfulness. Respecting academic dialogue partners is an aspect of love to neighbor disciplines.

While striving for academic excellence, doctoral programs should also be rooted in the absolute necessity of humility and total dependence on God. The pursuit of knowledge through autonomous human intelligence without reliance on God does not honour God. Doctoral students should seek God's help in all aspects of their lives and their education.

The connection between spiritual formation and research needs to be demonstrated in the supervisory/mentoring relationship. Supervisors of academic research projects should be committed to the personal modelling and the promotion of both academic excellence and its integration with spiritual formation.

Supervisors should model and inculcate values such as:
- honesty and intellectual rigour;
- a commitment to the truth wherever it leads;
- a humble willingness to acknowledge mistakes, misunderstandings, prejudices and presuppositions, and to value their correction;
- a commitment to research that demonstrates ethical and intellectual consistency;
- a dedication to serve the church through their own academic gifting and by developing the gifting of their students.

The prayer the Apostle Paul prays for the Philippians could be equally applicable to the Christian scholar: "And I pray this, that your love may abound even more and more in **knowledge and every kind of insight** so that you can decide what is best, and thus be sincere and blameless for the day of Christ, filled with the fruit of righteousness that comes through Jesus Christ to the glory and praise of God." (Phil 1:9–11)

9) Doctoral Programs Should Equip Students for Christian Leadership and Teaching Ministry

Doctoral programs should encourage the integration of thinking, learning, and action. They should equip students with skills that are specific to their academic discipline, but also with the skills of the self-managing learner that equip them for a life of independent research. High-grade skills in exercising critical judgment are essential for academic leadership. Where programs are designed to equip students for academic teaching and leadership, they should seek to integrate training in these areas into their structure.

During the course of doctoral studies students need to learn about project management, time management, communication skills, collaboration, teamwork, and administration, all of which are all key components of academic work.

Where the explicit aim is to produce scholars who will work in theological education, courses on academic teaching, administration, and leadership can be integrated into the doctoral program structure. These are especially successful when they include practical experience components that involve working with experienced mentors. Equipping doctoral students to deploy the academic knowledge they have gained in teaching and leadership contexts is an important aspect of the formation of scholars.

Doctoral students need to develop the skills that will enable them to be integrated and well-functioning members of the academic community or Christian organization where they will teach or lead in the future. They need to learn how to develop the practice of collegiality, a commitment to work for the enhancement of the institution and the needs of the churches it serves, as well as maintaining their own academic development.

10) Doctoral Programs Should Foster the Integration of Learning

All truth belongs to God, and is not limited by traditional boundaries that separate academic disciplines from one another. Integration of thinking reflects the Lordship of Christ over all reality.

Doctoral studies should promote depth of thinking and intellectual rigour, but also create in students the capacity to integrate what they learn. Students should learn to establish broader lines of connectedness across disciplines. They should be able to integrate the cutting edge of scholarship with their own research, and relate this to their own context. They need to be able to integrate their research findings with outcomes in theological training that serve the preparation of future Christian leaders.

11) Doctoral Programs Should Have Well-Functioning Academic Structures

Successful doctoral programs need more than good supervisors and students. They need to exist in a wider academic structure that is supportive and functioning well. Doctoral students should only be accepted into an environment that provides support for learning about, and doing, research, where research is already taking place, and a research culture exists.

Sadly, the experience of doctoral students is sometimes spoiled by poorly functioning academic processes and structures. When the academic process and structure do not enhance the experience of doctoral students they fail in their service to the wider Christian community, and do not honour God. In universities and seminaries in the West, as well as those in the Majority World, there are occasions when review boards are delayed for months. Information about academic results and progression is sometimes not communicated to students for long periods. Delays in the convening of exam boards are particularly difficult for a student who is ready to defend their thesis. Also frustrating for students is being accepted onto a doctoral program only to find that their supervisor/mentor has gone on study leave for many months. Best practice ensures that adequate structure and processes are in place to deal promptly with issues that arise.

Excellence involves putting in place effective arrangements to maintain appropriate academic standards and enhance the quality of postgraduate research degrees, designed to meet national and international standards.

Resources

Running a doctoral program involves a significant commitment of resources (faculty time, library resources, administrative support), and should only be undertaken if these resources can be sustained to a high level of quality throughout the duration of the program.

It is not good academic practice to initiate and run a program that has inadequate resources to be sustained. Nor is it fair to students, or honouring to God, to do so.

Structures and Regulations

Institutions running doctoral programs should create and maintain appropriate structures and procedures for maintaining academic standards and enhancing the quality of postgraduate research degrees. In the design of programs, close attention needs to be given to the development of well-structured academic processes. Programs should have appropriate national validation/accreditation, as well as maintaining external relationships with bodies, such as the ICETE Regional Associations. They should meet all requirements of these external agencies.

The structure and success of doctoral programs should be measured against appropriate internal and external indicators and targets.

Clear and readily available institutional regulations should be produced for each doctoral program, and these need to be regularly communicated to students and faculty members. These should be supplemented by accessible guidance in different subject areas.

Codes of practice for running doctoral programs should be a part of institutional regulations and course handbooks. These should be made available to all students and faculty members who are involved in such programs, and consistently implemented.

Provision of Faculty

It is important to ensure that there are appropriate numbers of qualified academic faculty members to deliver and sustain doctoral programs throughout the duration of each cohort cycle. This includes the provision of appropriate administrative support.

Any adjunct faculty who assist in the delivery of doctoral programs must be appropriately qualified and should undergo full orientation and training into their role in the program. Visiting faculty should understand the context in which they are invited to teach, and the specific purposes and ethos of the program to which they will contribute, and reflect this in their teaching and interaction with students.

Doctoral programs must always strive for best practice in their delivery, with regular assessments of appropriate mechanisms and regular training of faculty. Those running programs should continually evaluate the best ways of learning, including non-formal and non-traditional models, and develop approaches that ensure the academic excellence of doctoral degrees that are offered.

This involves regular training of academic faculty and the creation of an ongoing community of scholarly reflective practitioners.

Rationale and Progression of Skills

Each element of a doctoral program should have a clearly developed rationale and serve a clear purpose in the development of skills for doctoral study. Where taught components and non-assessed elements are included in doctoral program, they should be designed to consolidate and enhance skills required in the research component of the PhD program.

Academic Structures

Institutions should create and maintain clear and well-developed academic structures for the running of doctoral programs, including establishing an appropriate committee(s) for program oversight and decision making. The composition of such committee (s) needs to be decided by the institution. Terms of reference and lines of accountability must be clearly established within the organizational structure. Minutes and reports will be available for the scrutiny of the institution's academic leadership and external accrediting bodies. Where possible, doctoral committees should include both student and external representation. Decisions about student progression and continuance should not be vested in a single individual.

There should be robust record keeping procedures for doctoral programs. These need to be adequate in scope, legibly maintained, regularly updated, and archived with appropriate provision for their safe storage and preservation.

12) Doctoral Programs Should Have Well-Developed Processes for the Selection and Admission of Students to Programs

During the ICETE Beirut Process there was much discussion about the types of students evangelical institutions should accept onto their doctoral programs. It was decided that more than solely academic criteria should be applied. The doctorate is a vital training for Christian leadership roles, and so attention should be given at admission to the candidate's Christian standing and evidence of spiritual maturity. This is reflected in the Preamble to the *Beirut Benchmarks*.

- Those accepted onto doctoral programs in Christian educational institutions should be church members commended for faithful discipleship and recognized for their mature leadership, and commitment to transformational service in both church and society.

Academic Entry Criteria

Doctoral programs need to ensure that they only admit students who, in their previous studies, have demonstrated the required skills to succeed at doctoral level. It is neither fair to students, nor a good stewardship of financial and academic resources, to allow students to enter doctoral programs who have little likelihood of success.

The skills required to succeed at doctoral level will normally be demonstrated through a high level of success on a recognized and validated Masters program in an area related to the intended field of research.

Students accepted onto doctoral programs also need to be able to demonstrate evidence of ability to develop and apply ideas in a research context in their intended field of specialisation, as well as an ability to continue study in a self-directed or autonomous way.

- Doctoral programs may require applicants to demonstrate additional competencies appropriate to the nature of the program, such as skills in biblical languages, and high levels of competency in the language(s) in which the program is undertaken.
- Because of the integration between academic and professional skills in professional doctoral programs, candidates need to demonstrate before admission that they have professional competence through a specified period of ministry experience served subsequent to completion of their most recent theological degree.[16] Overall life-time ministry experience can be taken into consideration in reducing this minimum period.
- Normally doctoral programs make provision for students to serve a probationary period (usually at least one year), at the end of which continuation within the program is either confirmed or denied. Where progression is refused, a lower degree can be awarded in recognition of work undertaken.

Admissions Policy and Procedure

It needs to be clear both to applicants and to faculty who is eligible to apply for doctoral studies, and there needs to be transparency in decision making.

- The institution's admissions policy needs to be publicly available, clear, consistently applied and to demonstrate equality of opportunity.
- Admissions decisions need to involve at least two members of the institution's academic faculty, and they should have received appropriate training, advice and guidance in respect of selection and admissions procedures. This avoids any suggestion that a

---

16. Normally this is specified as at least three years' experience.

candidate has been given an unfair advantage, or has been unjustly refused admission. A clearly outlined decision-making process for applications enables the institution to ensure that admissions policies are fairly and equally applied, and the highest of standards are maintained.
- It is important to supply applicants with relevant information at each stage of the admissions process, and to communicate decisions to them clearly and promptly.

Candidacy for Dissertation/Thesis Component of Doctoral Programs

- Students must progress through the different stages of a doctoral program needs by means of a properly established process. Regular appropriate review mechanisms need to be created, and benchmarks against which progression decisions are made should be clearly established. The thesis/dissertation component of a doctoral degree requires the demonstration of the highest level of skills. Students should only be admitted to candidacy/registered for the thesis/dissertation component of a doctoral program after they have received training in research methods, and having produced a substantial research-based written work of at least 10,000 words.[17]

13) Doctoral Programs Should Ensure the Provision of Appropriate Study and Research Resources for the Level of Study

As the highest academic award, doctoral programs need to be equipped with the highest level of academic facilities and resources. This encompasses library resources (books and e-resources), IT systems, and the provision of research study rooms or carrels.

The library sits at the heart of the academic facilities needed to deliver a doctoral program. It needs to be adequately resourced, and senior library staff should be involved in decisions about commencing and maintaining a doctoral program. The library holdings of an institution starting or running

---

17. Examples of such research-based projects include a postgraduate Masters dissertation/thesis, or an extended research/thesis proposal. This work must demonstrate that the candidates have the skills to enable them to succeed at the doctoral level.

a doctoral program must be of a size and quality suitable to the needs of the program, and include high-level academic material in the language of instruction and other languages as appropriate. Where an institution offering a doctoral program is part of a wider institution that has large library resources, or unhindered access to wide resources locally can be guaranteed to students, investment in physical library resources may be on a lower scale, but high-quality library access must be ensured at all times. Where institutions accept students who study wholly or partly 'at-a-distance' through online or distributed-learning models, they must ensure those they admit will have adequate access throughout their programs to the size and level of library and other learning resources appropriate to doctoral-level education.

The suitability of library holdings cannot be measured solely by the quantity of its books. The available materials need to include publications at the cutting edge of current academic discourse, and leading research publications in the fields where doctoral supervision is offered.

Library Funding

Building a high quality library takes long-term strategic investment. If library funding is reduced for even a short period, it can take many years to restore holdings to previous levels. In view of the strategic position the library holds in creating a learning and research environment, this is a false economy. To guard against this, institutions with doctoral programs should set aside a minimum amount of the institution's annual operational income for library acquisitions and enhanced e-learning resources. These sums need to be firmly guaranteed. [18] The institution's leadership should establish an agreed figure for additional accessions to each specified field of doctoral studies.[19]

Library Collection Size and Quality

In order to provide an adequate research base for scholars, institutions offering doctoral programs need to create a library that is sufficiently large in number of volumes and scope of holdings to sustain high-level research

---

18. A minimum is 5% of the institution's annual operational income. The calculation should include as income any donated salaries of expatriate faculty.

19. The ACTEA doctoral programme review guidelines suggest a minimum of USD $1,000 a year for accessions in each specified field of study.

work.[20] Physical holdings of books should be supplemented through the holdings of titles in electronic format, but the institution needs to ensure that students have easy and ready access. Such permanently accessible electronic books can be included in the overall total of titles considered appropriate for a doctoral program.

In addition, research subscriptions to leading, peer-reviewed, academic journals should be maintained in the fields in which doctoral awards are offered, to enable students to demonstrate where their research fits with the up-to-date research of others.[21] These can include journals available through online databases by electronic subscription, although the importance of maintaining such subscriptions once established is clear. Quantity should not be pursued at the expense of consistent quality.[22] Journals and books that are not at an appropriate academic level should be avoided in acquisitions. The holdings of a library where research is to take place should demonstrate both breadth and concentration with reference to appropriate academic levels, theological orientations, and subjects covered.[23] To ensure that research is relevant to the context, significant attention should be given to acquiring materials that reflect the geographical and cultural situation of the institution, and the subjects of instruction at the institution. The reference collection and periodicals received should reflect a similar blend of general breadth and subject-specific concentration.

Borrowing Rights and Loans

To assist students with their research, doctoral students should have enhanced borrowing rights for written materials and interlibrary loan books.

Because a single library, even in large institutions, is rarely large enough to resource all doctoral students across a range of subject areas, libraries

---

20. For an institution delivering a doctoral program, its library should contain at least 40,000 titles, comprising up-to-date and research-led material. Where institutions have a smaller collection, 25,000 titles is considered an initial minimum, but within five years of a doctoral program starting, the total of 40,000 should be achieved.
21. Doctoral students should be able to access at least 100 journals in the theological disciplines.
22. Superficial and irrelevant titles should be eliminated from holdings, and not included in the initial baseline 40,000-volume library size.
23. The library should contain at least 2,000 volumes particular to each specified doctoral field, including a substantial portion of the major scholarly titles, reference materials, and journals (including back issue collections) in that field.

should ensure that doctoral students and research-active faculty also have access to the range of academic resources available in local, regional, and national academic libraries and centres of excellence in theological education and other disciplines. This should involve access to local university libraries, and regional and national libraries and, wherever possible, borrowing rights at these should be secured.

It is important that libraries in theological colleges should make provision for inter-library loan facilities for students. They should also make available on-site internet access to key collections held elsewhere. Where these arrangements to supplement on-site holdings are not available, libraries should substantially increase the size of their collection of books and journals in the area(s) of their specialization.

Other Key Issues

(a) As well as serving the immediate needs of its research students, a library should serve as a resource base where research can be conducted into specific topics that are particularly relevant to the local context. Libraries should establish and maintain collections of appropriate archives and primary source materials upon which such research can be undertaken. A number of evangelical institutions are making special collections of resources relating specifically to their respective regions.

(b) To enable ease of access to the collection by research scholars, libraries need to be adequately staffed so as to ensure proper and efficient running and maintenance. Library staff should include those with appropriate qualifications in librarianship and with an understanding of theological disciplines.

(c) In order to fully benefit from the resources available, students need to receive appropriate induction and regularly updated training in the use of both physical and electronic library resources. Relevant health and safety and legislative information should be supplied, together with materials dealing with issues such as information storage and usage, and copyright law.

(d) Materials should be catalogued using an internationally recognized catalogue system, and libraries should make catalogues available in electronically accessible format.

(e) Libraries should ensure that they maintain operating hours that are conducive to the working hours of research students.

(f) Library facilities and procedures should be adequate for preserving the holdings against special hazards arising from climate and insects.

(g) Because the length of the research undertaken by doctoral students is more extensive in terms of duration and size, the physical environment in which they work should be conducive to high-level study. The creation of designated study space, with appropriate secure storage facilities for their research materials within, or adjacent to, the library, greatly enhances the student research experience and is expected in institutions where doctoral study is taking place.

Information Technology Resources

In the light of the rapidly growing availability of resources that are often only available electronically, libraries need to ensure high-grade access to electronic and internet-based materials at levels suitable for intensive research-based study. Research students need to have access to computing equipment, and stable broadband internet connection enabling email, internet searching, electronic access to databases and electronic journals, and facility for downloading research materials. High quality internet access should be freely available to research students, who should receive training in the use of resources available.

Alongside high-grade Information Technology, library resources need to include up-to-date facilities for copying and electronically scanning research materials to enable students to access easily a wide range of material and store it in retrievable form for future use.

14) Doctoral Programs Should Have Well-Functioning Administrative and Financial Process

Doctoral students face significant distress when financial processes do not work well, when there is uncertainty about fee levels, or delays in releasing bursary funds, or funds deposited for their maintenance by sponsors.

Good supervision and facilities can all too easily be undermined by inadequacies in the finance office, or registration or administration processes. Complexities and delays in these areas can hamper the research progress of students, and significantly detract from the study experience of students. Excellence should be reflected at all levels and dimensions of the institution.

Fees

- Student fees for doctoral programs should be openly published each year, together with a statement of all other fees and dues that students are required to pay.
- Student fees need to be regularly reviewed, to make sure that they correlate with both the financial needs of the institution and with the financial abilities of the students and their sponsors. However, once a student is admitted to a program, the level of annual student fee and other dues should not be subjected to unexpected increases that would make it impossible to complete his or her course of study.

Financial Assistance to Students

- Many students find it difficult to afford the high cost over long periods of time that doctoral studies entail. Efforts should be made to provide scholarships or bursaries for those who are academically qualified for such study, but who would be disqualified from doing so because of financial disadvantage.
- Scholarship aid programs should be administered in keeping with written procedures. Decisions should be made on the basis of group consultation and not rest in the hands of a single person. Formal records of discussions held and action taken should be maintained to ensure proper accountability.

- All eligible students should be able to apply for scholarship aid when it is available. Scholarship opportunities from external bodies should also be freely publicized among eligible students.

15) Doctoral Programs Should Contain Appropriate Induction and Training Elements

The transition for students into research-based programs from those where study has been by means of assessed coursework can be very difficult. Some have little experience of autonomous learning and find it difficult to study independently. Providing doctoral students with appropriate academic advice and support at the beginning and throughout the duration of their programs is vital equipment for success in doctoral programs.

An induction program for new students should be run at the start of a doctoral program, reflecting the specific needs of doctoral students and providing appropriate information about the institution, its programs, codes of conduct, student responsibilities, facilities available, health and safety issues. Key information should also be presented in the form of a doctoral handbook. After initial induction, throughout the duration of the doctoral program, other research training opportunities should be provided at regular intervals in order to progressively build research and professional skills. This research-skills training should cover topics such as:

i. Understanding how learning happens at doctoral level

ii. Research methodology, and developing skills in epistemology, and meta-level reflection

iii. Building analytical and synthetic skills; framing research questions

iv. Written communication skills for the academic context, and for beyond the academic context

v. Research ethics, and approaches to human-subject research

vi. The Christian understanding of research and doctoral education, including the role of research within the kingdom of God

vii. Oral presentation and discourse skills –

- Giving research papers,
- Discussing the research findings of others

viii. ICT skills

ix. Bibliographic skills

x. Use of electronic resources and web-based materials

xi. Project planning and time management

xii. Record keeping and record management

Other skills for professional development and leadership in theological education also need to be taught, including:

i. Participation in seminars, workshops and academic conferences

ii. Preparation for examination

iii. Personal and career development, and future employment planning

iv. Utilizing the doctoral qualification after it has been completed. This should include -
   - Teaching and lecturing skills (pedagogy, andragogy)
   - Academic administration
   - Life after the doctorate – ongoing research, writing, integrating ongoing research into service for the Kingdom of God
   - Scholarship as life-long vocation
   - Theological education and mission
   - Writing for publication

16) Only Supervisors/Mentors/Thesis Advisors[24] Who Are Well Qualified and Well Trained Should Be Appointed

Supervising doctoral students in evangelical theological institutions is a crucial mentoring role. It is primarily an academic role, but it also contains certain aspects that have a pastoral dimension, although this should not interfere with the primary academic responsibilities. To do this those **who are supervisors need to be** established teachers and mature Christian leaders. They need to be able to model and guide the patterns of godly Christian scholarship, and be committed to both the academic and spiritual formation of those they supervise.

Supervisors

- Doctoral supervisors should be in good standing in the Christian academic community and in the local church.
- They should be capable of providing both academic support and demonstrating appropriate pastoral sensitivity to the needs of the student. Where the institution requires this, they will be willing to sign its statement of faith or confessional basis.
- They should have demonstrated the ability to integrate academic and spiritual excellence.
- Doctoral supervisors need to be appropriately qualified and have the appropriate experience, skills and subject knowledge to support, train and monitor the research students assigned to them.
- Supervisors or mentors of doctoral candidates need regular opportunities for faculty development and training.
- Research activity feeds into good academic supervision, so research supervisors need to maintain research-level academic currency as part of their faculty development activity.
- To avoid confusion about what is expected of the supervisory relationship, institutions need to ensure that the responsibilities of research supervisors are clearly communicated to supervisors and students through written guidance.

---

24. The term 'supervisor' is used in the UK, European and some Majority World programs. In other geographical contexts the term 'mentor', or 'thesis advisor', is used. These are to be understood as equivalent terms, with the strengths of each system included.

- The primary supervisor of a doctoral thesis/dissertation needs to be qualified to at least the doctoral level of the student they are supervising. They should have an earned research doctorate in the field in which the doctoral student intends to research, be an experienced supervisor of independent research, and have been teaching for several years. A supervisor needs to have expertise and academic currency in areas that closely match the intended research of the doctoral student. Evidence for this will be measured in terms of recent publications and research activity. Ideally institutions should have on their faculty supervisors who have earned their doctorates in a range of academic institutions.
- The student-supervisor relationship is crucial for the success of the student. Allocation of students to supervisors should be an institutional decision, but it should be made in consultation with the student and the intended supervisor. Institutions need to point out that it is in the student's best interest to identify the likely supervisor of an intended thesis/dissertation at the earliest opportunity.

Supervisory Teams

- Each doctoral student on the thesis/dissertation component of a doctoral program should have a minimum of one main supervisor, but she/he should normally be part of a supervisory team. This ensures that the student has access to the best range of expertise, and supervisors are there to support a student if a member of the team is on reach leave or unable to provide support for a period of time. There needs always to be one clearly identified point of contact within the supervisory team for the student. Normally the lead supervisor should be a member of academic faculty in the institution where the doctoral program is being delivered.
- Where a thesis/dissertation topic is clearly interdisciplinary, institutions should put together a supervisory team that is made up of individuals who have the required subject-specific specializations to match the needs of the research topic.
- Supervisory teams may include second supervisors who are not in possession of a doctorate. Such individuals need to be experienced teachers at postgraduate level with detailed and subject-specific

academic currency. Their role is to support the work of the main supervisor.
- Supervisory teams may also include members from other academic institutions, but those so appointed should have appropriate academic qualifications and research currency, and also demonstrate sympathy with the aims and ethos of the institution where the doctoral program is being offered.

Supervisory Arrangements

The details of supervisory relationships are a matter of individual negotiation between supervisor and student, but doctoral programs should have in place appropriate guidelines that establish the normal frequency and expected length of duration of supervisory sessions. These avoid misunderstandings about the level of support available, and create realistic expectations. [25]

Reporting by Supervisors

During the research stage of their programs, doctoral students can often feel uncertain about how much progress they are making, which can create insecurity and frustration. To assist students in their progression through a program, institutions need to have in place clearly defined mechanisms for monitoring and supporting the progress of doctoral students, including formal reviews and explicit review stages. This ensures realistic expectations and appropriate standards are established. These will involve both supervisors and students. Guidance should be provided to students, supervisors and others involved in monitoring progress and the regular review process. It is important to maintain appropriate records of the outcomes of meetings and reviews.

- The progress of doctoral students should normally be monitored formally at least once every six months, and annually for part-time students. The nature of such reviews should be such that they allow scope for feedback from students as to the quality of supervision they have received.

---

25. Normally full-time students would expect to see their supervisors at least once every two months, and part-time students three times a year. Where distance is a factor, various formats such as video conferencing, Skype, etc, can be used to supplement personal face-to-face meetings.

- The nature of each explicit review stage and its requirements should be clearly communicated by institutions in writing and in advance to students, supervisors, and others involved in progression reviews. It is important that students are informed promptly and in writing of the outcomes of formal reviews and stages of progression so that they do not face undue uncertainty or anxiety about their status within the program.
- Institutions offering doctoral programs must have in place appropriate mechanisms for dealing with formal and informal expressions of student feedback about supervision, including official complaints mechanisms. For disputes that cannot be resolved there should be provision for appeal to a final Third Party who is neutral and external to the institution, and who understands academic process.

Professional Development of Supervisors

Many supervisors are asked to take on the role without any formal training or preparation to supervise. Yet, such is the importance of good supervision to successful research work that institutions offering doctoral degrees need to put in place appropriate provisions for faculty development and training for supervisors of doctoral candidates.

Institutions also need to facilitate academic faculty engaged in doctoral supervision in maintaining research-level academic currency as part of their faculty development activity. Evidence of academic currency should be demonstrated through the publication of appropriate academic materials such as books, and academic journal articles and papers in their subject area, and attendance and presentation of papers at academic conferences. For many who are busy in academic teaching roles this is not easy. The maintenance of such academic currency needs to be supported by the provision of study days and periods of sabbatical leave free of teaching and administration.

17) Doctoral Research Degrees Should Only Be Offered Where a Research Culture and Supportive Institutional Environment Exists

Doctoral programs should only be run where a research culture has been established, and where research is encouraged. This is the proper context for research-based learning.

- It means that the institution running a doctoral program must value ideas, creative thinking, research activity and publication. Not only students but also supervisory faculty should be given regular opportunities to engage in research. There need to be opportunities for doctoral students to engage in peer-level academic debate. Publication of research work and conference participation should be encouraged.

Such an Institutional Research Culture normally includes such facilities as:

- The provision of formal induction and orientation for students entering doctoral programs, and ongoing training into research methods and skills, recognizing that doctoral education and research skills formation is part of an educational process.
- Regular (monthly would be a normal pattern) postgraduate seminars where students can present work and hear academic presentations from visiting scholars and their peer-group (or facility for conducting these gatherings in appropriate electronic or virtual formats).[26]
- Institutions offering academic doctoral programs need to demonstrate a pattern of engagement with the international network of doctoral-level scholarship in order to provide for breadth and enrichment of learning, cross-fertilization of ideas, and international comparability. This may include facilitating doctoral candidates in a period of residency outside their own national context during the program of their doctoral program, helping them to attend conferences and engage in international peer-level scholarly debate.

---

26. Some institutions have successfully run week-long research colloquia at which students present papers, and supervisors and invited academics participate.

18) *The Size and Structure of Doctoral Programs Needs to Be Appropriate to the Highest Level of Academic Study*

When students begin doctoral programs they need to know the expectations of them in terms of time and duration. The amount of time required for study must be realistic for students, especially if they study part-time while engaged in another form of ministry or where research is combined with ministry practice, as in the Professional Doctorate. Students also need to know the amount of written work that is expected of them and the form in which it is to be delivered.

Institutions need to have maximum registration periods for both full-time and part-time doctoral programs.[27]

The normal minimum registration period for a doctoral award is three years of full-time study. The normal minimum registration period for a part-time doctoral award is six years.[28]

Thesis/Dissertation

The thesis/dissertation in a doctoral program is an academic project that involves a sustained piece of writing based on research work.

The purpose of the thesis is to show the student's command of the area of knowledge and scholarship in the field in which research has been undertaken. It is designed to demonstrate the student's skills in analysis and evaluation of ideas and arguments. The thesis should contain the student's independent argument, which is documented from her or his own research findings and from scholarly secondary literature. The thesis argument should

---

27. For doctoral programs which include an initial taught and examined component (such as coursework and comprehensive examinations), the normal maximum registration period for the whole program will be eight years for full-time study and ten years for part-time study. For doctoral programs that are assessed entirely by a research-based thesis/dissertation, the normal maximum registration is five years for a full-time program and nine years for a part-time program.

28. A year of full-time study is normally calculated as 1,500–1,800 hours of study per year on a research doctoral program. Part-time study is calculated on an equivalent pro-rata basis. Many part-time students combine their studies with other ministry work, but they must ensure that they will have sufficient time to devote to their studies on a regular basis throughout the year. The institution of study must also ensure this provision has been securely established, and students must ensure that requisite time allowances for study are agreed with their employers. Doctorates can be successfully completed part-time, but not adequately in 'spare time'.
A professional doctorate program will normally involve a total of at least 2,700 hours of formal study across its duration in addition to ongoing in-service professional practice.

be presented in a sustained, well-structured and well-reasoned way, and its strengths evaluated. The work should be presented at a scholarly level that merits publication in whole or in part.

As one of the major components of the doctoral degree, institutions need to provide a minimum and a maximum word limit for the thesis. These need to be clearly communicated to students in written regulations and guidelines.[29]

Any requirements as to the presentation and formatting of doctoral theses/dissertations (including stylistic and referencing conventions) need to be communicated clearly to students in written regulations and guidance at the outset of their PhD programs. This will include guidance on the language (or languages) which can be used in the presentation of a thesis/dissertation, and whether translations of components in other languages will be included.

19) Institutions Should Have in Place Established Codes of Academic and Research Ethics

Demonstrating excellence in the area of academic and research ethics is part of our Christian calling to show excellence in all aspects of life. High standards of academic and research ethics are essential to the maintenance of global academic standards. As the 2010 Singapore Statement on Research Integrity puts it: "While there can be and are national and disciplinary differences in the way research is organized and conducted, there are also principles and professional responsibilities that are fundamental to the integrity of research wherever it is undertaken."

Similar statements on Research Ethics are found in the 2011 European Code of Conduct for Research Integrity.

---

29. The normal word limits for a research doctoral thesis/dissertation are between 75,000 to 100,000 words (or equivalent number of pages in specified format). Stipulations as to whether this total includes footnotes, bibliography and appendices will be set out in program regulations and guidance.

The normal word limit for the thesis/dissertation component in a professional doctorate degree is between 50,000 and 75,000 words (or equivalent number of pages in specified format). Together with assignments required in taught components of a professional doctorate, the overall total number of words (or equivalent pages) a student is required to submit for assessment in the program of a professional doctorate program will be similar to those on a research PhD program. Stipulations as to whether this total includes footnotes, bibliography and appendices need to be set out in program regulations and guidance.

The Singapore statement sets out fourteen key principles of Research Integrity:[30]

i. ***Integrity:*** this means that researchers need to take responsibility for the trustworthiness of their research.

ii. ***Regulations and Policies*** related to research should be closely adhered to.

iii. ***Research Methods:*** this means employing appropriate research methods, basing conclusions on critical analysis of the evidence and report findings and interpretations fully and objectively.

iv. ***Research Records:*** keeping clear, accurate records of all research, so that verification and replication of results can be made by other researchers.

v. ***Research Findings:*** data and findings should be shared openly and promptly.

vi. ***Authorship:*** Researchers should take responsibility for their contributions to all publications, funding applications, reports and other representations of their research.

vii. ***Publication Acknowledgement:*** Researchers should acknowledge in publications the names and roles of those who made significant contributions to the research, including writers, funders, sponsors, and others.

viii. ***Peer Review:*** Researchers should offer fair, prompt and rigorous evaluations when reviewing the work of others.

---

30. The "Singapore Statement on Research Integrity" was developed at the 2nd World Conference on Research Integrity, 21–24 July 2010, in Singapore, as a global guide to the responsible conduct of research. It is not a regulatory document and does not represent the official policies of the countries and organizations that funded and/or participated in the conference - www.singaporestatement.org
A full statement on Research Ethics and Integrity is found in the *European Code of Conduct for Research Integrity* produced by the European Science Foundation and the European Federation of National Academies of Sciences and Humanities, March 2011.

ix. **Conflict of Interest:** Researchers should disclose financial and other conflicts of interest that could compromise the trustworthiness of their work in research and writing.

x. **Public Communication:** Researchers should only comment professionally on areas within their recognized expertise engaged in public discussions about research findings, and distinguish professional comments from personal views.

xi. **Reporting Irresponsible Research Practices:** Researchers should report to the appropriate authorities any suspected research misconduct, such as fabrication, falsification or plagiarism, and any research practices that undermine the trustworthiness of research, such as carelessness, improperly listing authors, failing to report conflicting data, or the use of misleading analytical methods.

xii. **Responding to Irresponsible Research Practices:** Research institutions, journals, and professional organizations and agencies involved in supporting research should have procedures for dealing with allegations of misconduct and irresponsible research practices, and procedures for protecting those who report such behaviour in good faith. When misconduct in research is confirmed, appropriate actions should be taken promptly, including correcting the research record.

xiii. **Research Environments:** Research institutions should create and sustain environments that encourage integrity through appropriate education, clear policies, and reasonable standards for advancement.

xiv. **Societal Considerations:** Researchers and research institutions need to recognize that they have an ethical obligation to weigh societal benefits against the risks inherent in their work.

Plagiarism

Institutional regulations and program guidance need to set out clearly that all source material is to be acknowledged and fully referenced, and the form in which such references will be presented. Plagiarism reflects not only academic weaknesses, but also moral and spiritual failings. Warnings against plagiarism must be highlighted in institutional regulations and program guidance, together with details of the sanctions that will be imposed if plagiarism is detected in a doctoral thesis/dissertation.

Permissions

Any guidelines about material that is permitted, or not permitted, to be included in a thesis/dissertation (e.g. material from work previously published by the candidate) should be communicated clearly to students in written regulations and guidance at the outset of their PhD programs.

Proper permissions for the use of personal information or data from the subjects of research need to be obtained, and codes of research ethics followed with any material that involves human subjects of research.

20) Where Taught Components Exist in Doctoral Degrees They Must Have a Clear Rationale and Be Designed to Build Skills

A number of doctoral programs include coursework as part of their initial phase. These can have value in consolidating understanding, and opening up potential areas for future research. They need to be designed with a clear rationale so that they build knowledge and skills in preparation for the final research project.

- Where doctoral programs include a combination of taught courses and directed research, these must be designed so that they equip the student with a substantial mastery of the subject material, theory, bibliography, research, and methodology, across a significant portion of the field of specialization.
- Taught courses should seek to develop the student's capacity for independent thinking and making a creative contribution in their field of study, and with thorough understanding of relevant cognate fields sufficient for effectiveness in this field. In this way they build the skills for the major research project.
- Oral and/or written assessment methods (for example, comprehensive examinations) should be designed to develop the capacity for the critical thinking, evaluative skills, and independent and creative thinking required in the major research project component.

- Taught courses should build the skills doctoral students require to undertake a major, sustained, piece of academic research and writing, and for a future life of independent learning.

21) The Assessment and Examination of Doctoral Degrees Must Be Appropriate to the Highest Level of Academic Work

In his 2006 paper "Addressing the North-South Divide" delivered at the ICETE triennial at Chiang Mai, Chris Wright said: "It will do the world of evangelical scholarship and theological education no favours at all simply to inflate the currency at the doctoral level by flooding the market with sub-standard courses and awards. Let us be willing to invest in long-term quality and contextual excellence. This is where ICETE can play a major role in holding all its constituent parts to serious mutual accountability in this area."[31]

The *Beirut Benchmarks* were developed with this intention of creating high quality, internationally agreed, statements of what the doctorate should be like and what skills holders of the doctorate should demonstrate. When examining a doctoral thesis/dissertation, examiners need to ask the question: "If this doctoral thesis was offered for examination somewhere else in the world, would it be offered a doctoral award?"

Excellence in examination means ensuring that students are well prepared for that examination. It means utilizing properly qualified examiners who are leaders in their field. Examinations need to have a clearly established process and reporting structure to ensure that they are conducted properly. A correct understanding of the proper level of attainment required, and how to measure this, is needed.

Context may shape the form of examination. Some programs will be designed with a public examination in mind; others will include a private examination meeting with examiners. The size of examination panel may vary. Some examinations may not involve an oral component, whereas in other contexts that will be central to the process. Whatever the situation, excellence must be demonstrated in the level of the award, and the standard of the work examined must be shown to be the same as that produced by

---

31. Chris Wright, "Addressing the North-South Divide", Paper presented at ICETE triennial conference, Chiang Mai, 2006.

other successful doctoral candidates both nationally and internationally. Assessment standards, and all processes, must be transparent and fair.

a) Preparation

Institutions need to provide training and guidance to students during their doctoral programs to ensure that they are adequately prepared for the examination of their thesis/dissertation. This includes experience of confidently discussing and defending their work with their academic peers. This experience can be gained through taking opportunities for presentation of work at graduate seminars, academic conferences, pre-viva events, etc.

b) Progression

Criteria for progression within different stages of a doctoral program need to be clearly established in program regulations and communicated to students, and supervisors.

The place and purpose of components examined by written examination in the early stages of the doctoral program, such as comprehensive examinations, and their relationship to the final offer of a doctoral award, needs to be clearly explained in the program regulations.

c) The Examination

Institutions awarding doctoral degrees must have in place clear institutional regulations for the conducting of examinations.

Research degree examinations need to be carried out within a reasonable timescale, normally within three months of final thesis/dissertation submission. Criteria used to assess doctoral degrees also have to be clear and readily available to students, academic faculty and examiners.

In most cases the examination of a doctoral thesis/dissertation will include an oral component (defence) in which candidates have opportunity to discuss and be questioned in detail about their own work in person. Examiners must also have the opportunity to satisfy themselves that the work is the candidate's own. In cases where there is an oral component for the examination of the thesis/dissertation, clear guidelines for how this is conducted need to be put in place, and set out in the program documents. When distance is a factor for examiners or candidates, it is possible for an examination to be conducted by telephone or electronic/video means, so long as the performance of the candidate is not prejudiced by use of these means.

Institutions need to ensure that doctoral examinations are properly moderated and conducted with appropriate impartiality and academic rigour. Assessment procedures must be clear, rigorously operated, and fairly and consistently applied.

Examiners need to clearly understand the nature of their role within the doctoral examination process, and how final decisions about the granting of the academic award are arrived at. The institution needs to have clear guidelines and procedures in place for when there is a disagreement between examiners as to the result of a doctoral examination.

Fully developed reporting structures should be in place, and documentation available for examiners, which will include the opportunity for individual examiner comments. Report forms for examiners need to state clearly the criteria upon which the candidate is being examined. These should include the types of criteria established in the *Beirut Benchmarks*.

d) Outcomes

The range of possible outcomes for a doctoral examination need to be communicated clearly to candidates and examiners, and the criteria for each outcome set out in written form. Outcomes for examinations must be promptly communicated in both oral form and in writing to candidates by examiners, with clear instructions and guidance on any revisions to a thesis/dissertation that may be required.

Institutions that offer doctoral awards with different classifications (e.g. *cum laude, magna cum laude)*, need to have fully developed written criteria for these different levels, which are made available to both students and examiners.

e) Examiners

Institutions should establish procedures outlining the composition, appointment, and responsibilities of examining panels for doctoral theses.

Institutions should ensure that examination panels for doctoral degrees are comprised of members with the skills that ensure a national and international equivalence of standards across the university/higher education sector. For this reason, institutions should have in place examination processes for doctoral degrees that normally include external examiner representation.[32]

Institutions must make sure that doctoral examination panels are comprised of appropriately qualified examiners. Normally, they will all be holders of earned research doctoral awards, and be research-active. Those appointed external examiners need to have the required subject expertise, be scholars of international standing, be research-active and have major and current publications in the area being examined.

Where doctoral examinations are conducted in evangelical academic contexts, the institution should ensure that examination panels are made up of members who have an understanding of the theological perspective of the institution and the candidate, and an ability to ensure that the thesis/dissertation itself is examined purely on its academic merits.

It is proper academic ethics to ensure that examiners declare at the outset any personal interest in the candidate. If they are planning to employ the candidate, or planning to publish with the candidate, or if they have, or have had, any close personal or family relationship with the candidate, they should not normally be part of the examination panel.

Examination panels for professional doctorates need to include those with subject-specific knowledge gained through holding a research-based PhD in the subject area, together with those who hold professional doctorates, and those who have extensive experience as reflective practitioners and are experienced professional leaders in the field.

f) Communication of Examination Results

Where examination results are confirmed by a higher degrees committee within the institution, any decision communicated by the examining panel is normally only provisional. Institutions must have in place clear policies concerning the relationship between the examining board, and the higher body that confirms the award, and regulations for resolving any disputes. Institutions need to ensure that these processes operate smoothly, and decisions are quickly communicated to the candidate.

---

32. An external examiner is someone who is not regularly employed by the institution where the doctoral research has been undertaken, and has not been involved in the supervision of the research student.

Details of ICETE Doctoral Initiative

ICETE Doctoral Initiative Advisory Council

The ICETE Doctoral Initiative Advisory Council (DIAC) is comprised of international educators experienced in evangelical theological higher education.

Members:

Carver Yu, China Graduate School of Theology (CGST), Hong Kong
Chris Wright, Langham Partnership (LP), UK
David Baer, Overseas Council (OC), USA
Havilah Dharamraj, South Asia Institute of Advanced Christian Studies (SAIACS), Bangalore, India
Las Newman, Caribbean Graduate School of Theology (CGST), Jamaica
Parush Parushev, International Baptist Theological Seminary (IBTS), Netherlands
Paul Bowers, International Council for Evangelical Theological Education (ICETE), USA/Africa
Paul Sanders, International Council for Evangelical Theological Education (ICETE), France
Ralph Enlow, Association for Biblical Higher Education (ABHE), USA
Riad Kassis, ICETE/Langham Partnership
Sergiy Sannikov, Euro-Asian Accrediting Association (E-AAA), Ukraine
Tite Tiénou, Trinity International University, US
Nupanga Weanzana wa Weanzana, Faculté de Théologie Évangélique de Bangui (FATEB)

ICETE Doctoral Initiative Steering Committee

The ICETE Doctoral Initiative Steering Committee is comprised of international educators experienced in evangelical theological higher education who have been part of previous ICETE Doctoral Initiative consultations.

Co-moderators:

Jung-Sook Lee, Torch Trinity Graduate University, South Korea
Ian Shaw, Langham Partnership, UK

Members:

Theresa Lua, Asia Graduate School of Theology (AGST), Philippines
Bernhard Ott, European Evangelical Accrediting Association (EEAA), Switzerland/Germany
Bulus Galadima, Nigeria and Biola University, USA
Evan Hunter, ScholarLeaders International, USA
Melody Mazuk, Director of Library Development, reSource Leadership International, Canada/USA
Scott Cunningham, Overseas Council (OC), USA

ICETE

International Council for Evangelical Theological Education
strengthening evangelical theological education through international cooperation

ICETE is a global community, sponsored by nine regional networks of theological schools, to enable international interaction and collaboration among all those engaged in strengthening and developing evangelical theological education and Christian leadership development worldwide.

The purpose of ICETE is:
1. To promote the enhancement of evangelical theological education worldwide.
2. To serve as a forum for interaction, partnership and collaboration among those involved in evangelical theological education and leadership development, for mutual assistance, stimulation and enrichment.
3. To provide networking and support services for regional associations of evangelical theological schools worldwide.
4. To facilitate among these bodies the advancement of their services to evangelical theological education within their regions.

Sponsoring associations include:

Africa: Association for Christian Theological Education in Africa (ACTEA)

Asia: Asia Theological Association (ATA)

Caribbean: Caribbean Evangelical Theological Association (CETA)

Europe: European Evangelical Accrediting Association (EEAA)

Euro-Asia: Euro-Asian Accrediting Association (E-AAA)

Latin America: Association for Evangelical Theological Education in Latin America (AETAL)

Middle East and North Africa: Middle East Association for Theological Education (MEATE)

North America: Association for Biblical Higher Education (ABHE)

South Pacific: South Pacific Association of Evangelical Colleges (SPAEC)

www.icete-edu.org

Langham Literature and its imprints are a ministry of Langham Partnership.

Langham Partnership is a global fellowship working in pursuit of the vision God entrusted to its founder John Stott –

> *to facilitate the growth of the church in maturity and Christ-likeness through raising the standards of biblical preaching and teaching.*

Our vision is to see churches in the majority world equipped for mission and growing to maturity in Christ through the ministry of pastors and leaders who believe, teach and live by the Word of God.

Our mission is to strengthen the ministry of the Word of God through:
- nurturing national movements for biblical preaching
- fostering the creation and distribution of evangelical literature
- enhancing evangelical theological education

especially in countries where churches are under-resourced.

Our ministry

Langham Preaching partners with national leaders to nurture indigenous biblical preaching movements for pastors and lay preachers all around the world. With the support of a team of trainers from many countries, a multi-level programme of seminars provides practical training, and is followed by a programme for training local facilitators. Local preachers' groups and national and regional networks ensure continuity and ongoing development, seeking to build vigorous movements committed to Bible exposition.

Langham Literature provides majority world preachers, scholars and seminary libraries with evangelical books and electronic resources through publishing and distribution, grants and discounts. The programme also fosters the creation of indigenous evangelical books in many languages, through writer's grants, strengthening local evangelical publishing houses, and investment in major regional literature projects, such as one volume Bible commentaries like *The Africa Bible Commentary* and *The South Asia Bible Commentary*.

Langham Scholars provides financial support for evangelical doctoral students from the majority world so that, when they return home, they may train pastors and other Christian leaders with sound, biblical and theological teaching. This programme equips those who equip others. Langham Scholars also works in partnership with majority world seminaries in strengthening evangelical theological education. A growing number of Langham Scholars study in high quality doctoral programmes in the majority world itself. As well as teaching the next generation of pastors, graduated Langham Scholars exercise significant influence through their writing and leadership.

To learn more about Langham Partnership and the work we do visit **langham.org**